Native Americans

Plains Indians

Mir Tamim Ansary

Heinemann Library
Chicago, Illinois

Printed in Hong Kong
Designed by Depke Design

04 03 02 01
10 9 8 7 6 5 4 3 2

Library of Congress Cataloging-in-Publication Data
Ansary, Mir Tamim.
        Plains Indians / Mir Tamim Ansary.
            p. cm. — (Native Americans)
        Includes bibliographical references and index.
        Summary: Describes the traditional way of life of the Plains
Indians and the changes brought to it by Europeans, discussing
homes, clothing, games, crafts, and beliefs.
        ISBN 1-57572-929-6 (library binding)
        1. Indians of North America-Great Plains Juvenile literature.
    [1. Indians of north America-Great Plains.] I. Title.
    II. Series: Ansary, Mir Tamim. Native Americans.
    E78.G73A567 2000
    978.004'97-dc21   99-37137
                                                           CIP

Acknowledgments
The author and publishers are grateful to the following for permission to reproduce copyright material:
Cover: Stock Montage, Inc.
AP/Wide World Photos, p. 30 top and bottom; Henry Bradshaw/Photo Researchers, Inc., p. 19; The Bridgeman Art
Library, p. 7; Buffalo Bill Historical Center, p. 21; Edward S. Curtis/National Geographic Image Collection, p. 14; Phil
Degginger, p. 4; The Granger Collection, pp. 8, 10, 11, 15, 16, 24, 25, 26; Tom McHugh/Photo Researchers, Inc., p. 9;
North Wind Pictures, pp. 12, 17, 18, 27, 29; The Philbrook Museum of Art, p. 22; Stock Montage, Inc., p. 13; Index Stock
Photography, p. 20; Daniel Westergren/National Geographic Image Collection, p. 28.

Every effort has been made to contact copyright holders of any material reproduced in this book. Any omissions will be
rectified in subsequent printings if notice is given to the publisher.

Our special thanks to Lana Grant, Native American MLS, for her
help in the preparation of this book.

Note to the Reader Some words are shown in bold, **like this.** You can find
out what they mean by looking in the glossary.

Contents

The Plains Region. 4

People of the Plains. 6

The Buffalo. 8

Living on the Move 10

Earth Lodge and Tipi 12

Plains Clothes. 14

Chiefs and Warriors. 16

War and Trade 18

Spirits and Medicine Bundles. 20

Tribal Gatherings 22

The Plains Wars 24

Victory and Defeat 26

The 20th Century 28

Famous Plains Indians 30

Glossary *31*

More Books to Read *32*

Index *32*

The Plains Region

The middle of North America is a huge plain. It stretches between the Rocky Mountains in the west and the Mississippi River in the east. Rolling hills form its edges, but the center is flat. As a Comanche Indian once said of this land, "There is nothing to break the light of the sun."

Today, the Plains are rich farmland. Long ago, however, this whole region was covered with wild grass. In the northeastern area, called the prairie, the grass grew taller than an adult man. In the center, where the land is flat, the grass was short. There, more than 60 million buffalo once roamed.

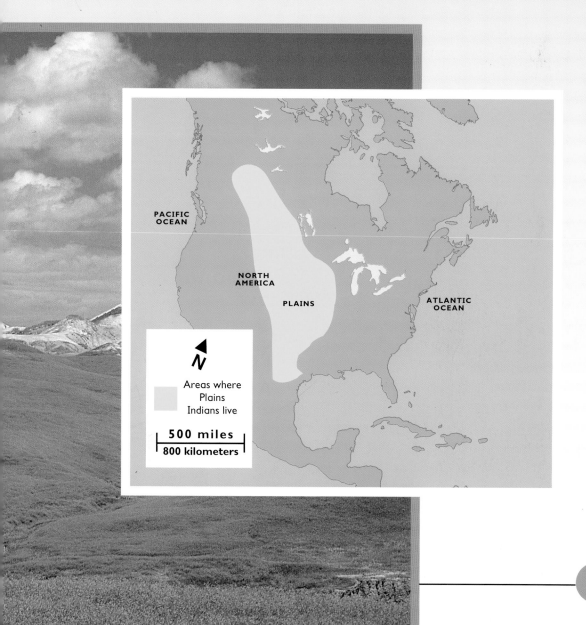

PACIFIC
OCEAN

NORTH
AMERICA

PLAINS

ATLANTIC
OCEAN

N

Areas where
Plains
Indians live

500 miles
800 kilometers

People of the Plains

Until the 1500s, people lived mainly on the edges of the Plains or along rivers. In the far west, for example, were the Blackfoot. In the northeast, tribes such as the Mandan had villages. They raised crops from fall through spring. In summer, they roamed the Plains in search of buffalo.

Hudson Bay

PACIFIC
OCEAN

Mandan

Crow

Sioux

Pawnee

Arapaho

NORTH
AMERICA

Cheyenne

N

Areas where
Plains
Indians live

500 miles
800 kilometers

Europeans changed all this. The Spanish brought horses to North America in the 1500s. The British brought guns and war. The British pushed Indians from other areas across the Mississippi River and onto the Plains. Once tribes, such as the Sioux, captured horses, they gave up farming. They became full-time **nomadic** hunters.

ATLANTIC OCEAN

The Dakota people moved onto the Plains after they got horses.

The Buffalo

These new **nomadic** tribes built their way of life around the buffalo. They ate buffalo meat, either boiled, broiled, or raw. They made buffalo blood into a pudding. They pounded dried buffalo meat together with fat and wild cherries. This was pemmican, a food that did not easily spoil. It could be eaten months after it was made.

A single buffalo herd could have half a million animals.

Tipi skins made of buffalo hides could last as long as 25 years.

The buffalo was used for much more than food. The Plains Indians made saddles, tents, and clothing from its skin. They made cups and spoons from its horns. They made toys and tools out of its bones. Its stomach became a bag. Every part of the buffalo was used for something. The Plains Indians even used buffalo **dung** as fuel for their fires.

Living on the Move

Buffalo were always on the move. So the hunters had to move, too. Before the 1500s, this was hard for the Indians. They had only dogs to drag their goods. They couldn't carry much. And getting close to buffalo on foot was hard. They hunted buffalo mostly by herding them over cliffs.

Before they had horses, the Plains Indians hunted buffalo on foot.

*Horses became so important to the Plains Indians
that most children learned to ride by the age of five.*

On horseback, however, hunters could charge close
to the buffalo. A band of families could follow a
herd. Horses carried everything the Indians needed
for a rich, full life. The Plains Indians spent much
time catching, buying, or stealing horses because
their way of life depended on this animal.

Earth Lodge and Tipi

Part-time farmers, such as the Mandan and Pawnee, lived in a type of house called an earth lodge. An earth lodge was partly underground. It was usually round and had a **dome**-shaped roof made of clay and grass. The roof was strong enough for a person to stand on.

A Mandan village might have about 60 earth lodges like these.

Smoke from the fire inside a tipi came out through a hole at the top, where you see the poles.

Nomads such as the Sioux and Crow lived in tipis. These roomy cone-shaped tents were made of buffalo hides. A tipi could be taken down or put up in minutes. It was warm in winter and cool in summer. Women owned the tipis and all the household goods inside them.

Plains Clothes

Men usually owned their clothes and weapons and not much more. A man's greatest **possession** was his buffalo hide shield. The shield was painted with images from the man's dreams. On special days, great warriors wore feather **bonnets,** too. Each feather stood for a brave deed the man had done in war.

The bonnets these men are wearing show that they are respected warriors.

Sometimes a person's head was painted red where the hair was parted.

On most days, both men and women of the Plains
wore leather leggings and a shirt or dress. In
summer, men usually wore only a **breechcloth.**
Both men and women wore their hair down to
their shoulders, loose or in braids. The hair was
parted down the middle.

Chiefs and Warriors

Any boy could grow up to be a chief. But he had to earn the title. He had to prove his courage in war and his wisdom when he spoke. He had to win respect by helping those in need. Only a brave, wise, and generous man could be chief.

A chief was a brave man who gave wise advice. A tribe could have more than one chief.

16

These Comanche and Arapaho warriors are having a war council.

The bravest men belonged to special warrior's clubs. These groups had colorful names. The Cheyenne, for example, had the Dog Soldiers. The warrior clubs acted as police for their tribes. They kept order on hunts, too. Many wore special outfits and followed their own strict rules.

War and Trade

The Plains tribes made war with one another, but it was not what Europeans called war. They did not try to **conquer** their enemies. They had no armies. Plains Indians made war to get horses and to prove personal courage. The greatest honor came from *counting coup*. This meant touching an enemy's body during battle without hurting him.

After a battle, Plains warriors met to talk about their deeds. Lying in such a meeting was considered very shameful.

Black Elk, a Lakota medicine man, shows how to say "my heart" in sign language.

Trade was constant, too, even though many of these tribes spoke different languages. People of different tribes could talk to each other using sign language. Almost everyone knew this special language—and it *was* a language. People could tell stories and have long conversations in the sign language of the Plains peoples.

Spirits and Medicine Bundles

Religious ideas were important in everyday life. According to these beliefs, everything has a living **spirit.** The sun, for example, is a mighty living power. Each of the four compass directions has a spirit. The earth is the mother of all spirits. And above all is *Wakan Tanka*—the Great Spirit.

This man is from the Omaha tribe.

This is what a typical medicine bag looks like.

Many people made "medicine bundles" to keep themselves connected to spirits. A medicine bundle is a small bag with several secret items, such as feathers or bones. Each item has a special meaning or importance to its owner. The owner believes that each item is something that will please his or her special spirits.

Tribal Gatherings

About once a year, a whole tribe would gather in one place. There, hundreds or even thousands of people would perform a group **ceremony**. This ceremony was meant to keep the tribe **united** and connected to the **spirit** world. The Cheyenne and others called their ceremony the Sun Dance.

At a Sun Dance, secret religious ceremonies take place in a round tipi, like the one you see here.

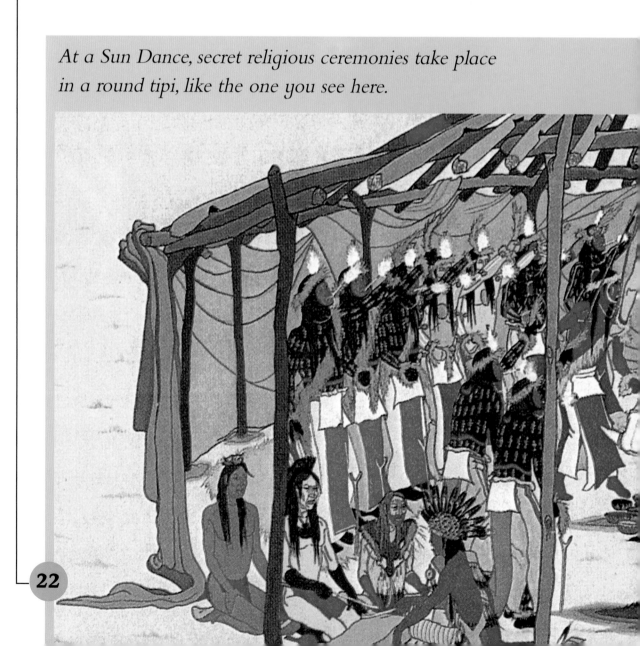

The Sun Dance is still performed by Plains Indians. At a Sun Dance, people form a circle around a **sacred** object. They move their feet slowly for two to four days, never stopping to eat, drink, or sleep. Through this hardship, they believe, they earn the protection of powerful spirits.

The Plains Wars

The **nomadic** buffalo hunters' way of life lasted about 100 years. By the 1830s, White settlers were moving west. These people took land from the Native Americans. They brought diseases to the Plains. Then White hunters started killing millions of buffalo. By the middle 1870s, they had wiped out the herds the Indians needed.

Railroad companies hired hunters to kill buffalo so the herds would not slow down the trains.

Red Cloud led a fight to claim the northern Plains for the Sioux people.

The Plains tribes struggled to save their way of life. The Oglala Sioux fought for the lands that are now North and South Dakota. In 1868, the U.S. government signed a **treaty** with the Sioux chief Red Cloud. The treaty promised the Dakota lands to the Sioux as one great Sioux **reservation.**

Victory and Defeat

In 1874, however, gold was found in the Black Hills of South Dakota. So Lieutenant Colonel George Custer was sent to remove the Indians. But Cheyenne, Sioux, and Arapaho warriors united against him. In 1876, Native American warriors led by Sitting Bull, Crazy Horse, and others, destroyed Custer's forces at the Battle of Little Big Horn.

This picture is part of a painted hide that shows the Battle of Little Big Horn. It was painted by Red Horse, a Sioux Chief.

The Plains Indians were forced to give up the lands they had once roamed.

This victory only brought more U.S. soldiers to the Plains. In 1889, the Great Sioux **Reservation** was split into six smaller ones. That year, Sitting Bull was murdered near his home on the Standing Rock Reservation. In December, U.S. soldiers killed a band of unarmed Sioux at Wounded Knee, South Dakota. The Plains Indians never went to war again.

The 20th Century

Today, the Plains Indians have **reservations** in many states, including Oklahoma, the Dakotas, and Montana. Modern Indians, however, honor their ancestors who once roamed the Plains. Indians of many tribes have **adopted** their dances, clothes, and other customs. You can see this at any powwow.

A huge statue of the Oglala Sioux chief Crazy Horse is being carved out of a mountain in South Dakota. This model shows what the sculpture will look like. The real statue is in the background.

These Kiowa Indians are performing a slow war dance at a powwow to celebrate Native American culture.

A powwow is a fair that brings together Indians of many tribes. This custom has spread across the nation. At powwows, Indian families gather to have fun, but also to explore what they share. In the movement to build one **united** Native American community, Plains Indians are among the leaders.

Famous Plains Indians

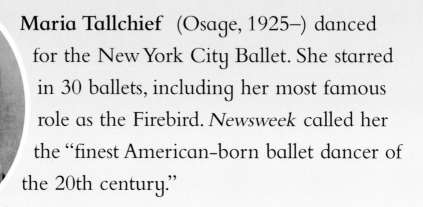

N. Scott Momaday (Kiowa, 1934–) is a poet, writer, and painter. His first novel *House of Dawn* won the Pulitzer Prize, the most important writing prize in America. His second book is an autobiography, *The Way to Rainy Mountain.* It is often taught in schools.

Maria Tallchief (Osage, 1925–) danced for the New York City Ballet. She starred in 30 ballets, including her most famous role as the Firebird. *Newsweek* called her the "finest American-born ballet dancer of the 20th century."

Black Elk (Lakota, 1863?–1950) was a famous healer, medicine man, and prophet. In 1930, he told his visions to the poet John Neihardt. The result was *Black Elk Speaks,* one of the most important books of Native American spiritual thought ever published.

Glossary

adopted took on as their own

ancient having to do with times long ago

bonnet hat or head covering

breechcloth piece of cloth worn around the hips and through the legs

ceremony set of acts done a special way, often having religious meaning

conquer to win or take something by force, usually land

dome round roof shape like an upside-down bowl

dung solid animal waste, or droppings

generous quick to give or share; unselfish

image any picture or pattern that can be imagined

nomadic having no fixed home; moving from place to place, usually to find a good source of food

performed to have done something

possession something that is owned

reservation land set aside for Native Americans

sacred given great respect, often for religious reasons

spirit unseen living force with a personality

treaty agreement made between countries or groups of people

united joined together

More Books to Read

Greene, Carol. *Black Elk: A Man with a Vision.* Danbury, Conn: Children's Press, 1990.

Greene, Jacqueline D. *Powwow: A Good Day to Dance.* Danbury, Conn: Franklin Watts, 1998.

Lund, Bill. *The Sioux Indians.* Danbury, Conn: Children's Press, 1997.

Index

Arapaho 6, 17, 24

Black Elk 19, 30
Black Hills 24
Blackfoot 4
buffalo 5, 6, 8, 9, 10, 11, 12, 13, 24

Cheyenne 6, 17, 20, 24
clothes 12, 13, 26
Comanche 4, 17
Crazy Horse 26, 28
Crow 6, 12
Custer, George 24

Dakota 7, 25
Dog Soldiers 17

gold 24
government 24
Great Sioux Reservation 25, 27
Great Spirit 20

Kiowa 28

Lakota 18, 30
Little Big Horn, Battle of 26

Mandan 6, 10
medicine man 19, 30
Mississippi River 4, 7
Momaday, N. Scott 30
Montana 26

Neihardt, John 30
nomads 13

Oglala 28
Osage 30

Pawnee 6, 10
pemmican 8
powwow 28, 29

Red Cloud 25
religion
reservation 25, 27

settlers 22
shield 12
sign language 19
Sioux 6, 7, 13, 25, 26, 27, 28
Sitting Bull 26, 27
soldiers 17, 27
South Dakota 24, 25, 27, 28
Sun Dance 22, 23

Tallchief, Maria 30
tipis 13
tools 9
toys 9
treaties 25

Wakan Tanka 20
warriors 14, 16, 17, 18, 26
Wounded Knee 27

Life